KU-099-348

Learn to Say No!

Smoking

Angela Royston

Heinemann
LIBRARY

Schools Library and Information Service

S00000630378

H www.heinemann.co.uk
Visit our website to find out more information about **Heinemann Library** books.

To order:
☎ Phone 44 (0) 1865 888066
▤ Send a fax to 44 (0) 1865 314091
▣ Visit the Heinemann Bookshop at www.heinemann.co.uk to browse our catalogue and order online.

First published in Great Britain by Heinemann Library,
Halley Court, Jordan Hill, Oxford OX2 8EJ
a division of Reed Educational and Professional Publishing Ltd.
Heinemann is a registered trademark of Reed Educational & Professional Publishing Ltd.

OXFORD MELBOURNE AUCKLAND
JOHANNESBURG BLANTYRE GABORONE
IBADAN PORTSMOUTH (NH) USA CHICAGO

© Reed Educational and Professional Publishing Ltd 2001
The moral right of the proprietor has been asserted.

All rights reserved. No part of this publication may be reproduced, stored in a retrieval system, or transmitted in any form or by any means, electronic, mechanical, photocopying, recording, or otherwise without either the prior written permission of the Publishers or a licence permitting restricted copying in the United Kingdom issued by the Copyright Licensing Agency Ltd, 90 Tottenham Court Road, London W1P 0LP.

Designed by AMR
Illustrations by Art Construction
Originated by Ambassador
Printed in Hong Kong/China

05 04 03 02 01
10 9 8 7 6 5 4 3 2 1

ISBN 0431 09906 5
This title is also available in a hardback library edition (ISBN 0 431 09901 4)

British Library Cataloguing in Publication Data
Royston, Angela
 Smoking. – (Learn to say no)
 1.Smoking – Health aspects – Juvenile literature 2.Tobacco
 – Physiological effect – Juvenile literature 3.Smoking –
 Law and legislation – Juvenile literature 4.Tobacco habit –
 Juvenile literature
 I.Title
 362.2'96

Acknowledgements
The Publishers would like to thank the following for permission to reproduce photographs:
Advertising Archives, pp.8, 15, 18; Eye Ubiquitous, pp.21, 26; Gareth Boden, pp.4, 10, 20, 24, 27; Image Bank, p.7 (Gabriel Covian), p.29 (Borros & Borros); Rex Features, p. 19; Ronald Grant Archive, p.9; Science Photo Library, p.17 (A Glauberman); Tony Stone Images, p.6 (Tom Raymond), p.13 (Ken Whitmore), p.14 (Robert Brons/BPS), p.22 (U.H.B. Trust), p.23 (David Glick), p.28 (David Madison); Topham Picturepoint, p.11.

Cover photograph reproduced with permission of Tony Stone and Sally & Richard Greenhill

Every effort has been made to contact copyright holders of any material reproduced in this book. Any omissions will be rectified in subsequent printings if notice is given to the Publisher.

Contents

DUDLEY PUBLIC LIBRARIES

L   457 10

630378   SCH

J 613. 85

Any words appearing in the text in bold, **like this**, are explained in the glossary.

What are drugs?

A drug is any substance that affects your body and changes the way you feel. There are three groups of drugs – **medicines**, **legal drugs** and **illegal drugs**.

Medicines

Many medicines, such as cough medicines and painkillers, help to soothe the symptoms of a disease. Other medicines, such as antiseptic cream and antibiotics, tackle the disease itself. Some medicines can only be **prescribed** by doctors, but others can be bought from a chemist or from shops such as supermarkets.

Coffee, tea and cola all contain caffeine, a legal drug that makes the heart beat faster and so makes you feel more awake.

Illegal or legal?

Legal drugs include medicines, of course, but the term usually refers to drugs such as alcohol and tobacco. These drugs affect the way a person feels but are not illegal for adults. Tea, coffee and cola are legal drugs too. Illegal drugs include **cannabis**, heroin, Ecstasy and LSD, and are forbidden by law.

Tobacco

This book tells you about tobacco and how it damages the body. It looks at why people smoke and why they often find it difficult to stop. It will give you plenty of reasons not to start smoking in the first place.

Did you know?

Tobacco is both a **stimulant** and a **depressant**. Apart from medicines, drugs are stimulants, depressants or **hallucinogens**.

A stimulant, such as caffeine in coffee or **nicotine** in tobacco, makes your heart and other organs work faster. A depressant makes a person relax. Nicotine in tobacco blocks the nerve signals in the brain and so makes the smoker feel relaxed. A hallucinogen, such as cannabis, alters the way a person sees or hears things.

Cigarettes may look harmless but each is packed with poisonous chemicals.

What is tobacco?

Tobacco leaves
Tobacco is the dried leaves of the tobacco plant. Tobacco grows well in warm and hot parts of the world and is often grown on huge farms owned by tobacco companies.

Tobacco leaves are harvested when fully ripe and then hung up to dry. They are **cured** and stored for two to three years before the tobacco is made into cigarettes, cigars or sold loose.

Cigarettes and loose tobacco
Cigarettes are usually made from different kinds of tobacco blended together, along with other ingredients to flavour it, such as honey, liquorice, menthol or sugar. Loose tobacco is smoked in a pipe or chewed, or rolled up by the smoker into a cigarette.

In the United States and Canada tobacco is usually harvested by machine, but in most other countries it is picked by hand.

Tobacco industry

China grows more tobacco than any other country. The United States is the world's second largest producer. Tobacco is also grown in India, Brazil, Turkey, Greece, Italy, Indonesia and Zimbabwe. The tobacco industry is very important in the United States. There are about 130,000 tobacco farms in the country and the industry provides many jobs, particularly in the southern states.

Big business

US tobacco companies sell huge amounts of tobacco and cigarettes to other countries. Fewer people in North America, western Europe and Australasia now smoke, but the tobacco companies have not suffered. They have found new customers in Russia, eastern Europe and Asia.

After harvesting, the tobacco leaves are hung up on sticks or strings and cured. Curing dries the leaves and changes their colour.

Talking point

In the United States the government helps tobacco farmers by guaranteeing them a fixed price for their crop. Do you think the US government should help an industry that employs thousands of workers but each year kills over 450,000 people in the US alone?

An old habit

Ancient smokers
Tobacco grows naturally in North and South America. The Mayans of Central America were smoking it over 2000 years ago and the **habit** gradually spread north to Native American tribes.

New World discovery
When explorers from Europe reached the New World (North and South America) about 500 years ago, they discovered new plants, including potatoes, sweetcorn and tobacco.

Cigarettes for sale
At first, tobacco was mainly smoked in pipes or rolled by hand into loose cigarettes. Then, just over 100 years ago, the first cigarette-making machine was invented. Cigarettes became cheap to produce and the tobacco companies began to persuade men to take up smoking. Their advertisements showed tough-looking men smoking. From the 1930s onwards advertisements also showed sophisticated women smoking.

This advertisement was produced in 1954. It links glamour and success with smoking cigarettes.

Many soldiers began to smoke during World War I. The British government bought vast quantities of cigarettes and gave them away free to the soldiers in the trenches. Millions of soldiers were killed fighting, but those that survived were **addicted** to smoking, and the number of deaths due to lung disease began to increase dramatically.

Dangers revealed

In the 1950s several studies showed not only that smoking cigarettes causes **lung cancer** but that it causes **heart disease**, too. The cigarette companies refused to admit that smoking is dangerous. It was only in the 1990s that the tobacco industry finally admitted that smoking is unhealthy.

The film star Rita Hayworth, photographed with a cigarette in her hand. Whereas smoking had been considered vulgar for women before World War I, in the 1930s it became a sign of sophistication. People now know better.

Did you know?

Some governments encourage people not to smoke. One way of doing this is to put a large **tax** on tobacco. Over three-quarters of the cost of a packet of cigarettes in Britain is tax. In 1997 taxes on tobacco raised over £10,000,000,000. The more money the government gets in this way, however, the more it would lose if everyone stopped smoking.

King James I

Sir Walter Raleigh introduced tobacco and pipe-smoking to England in 1586. James I was not impressed. In 1603 he wrote *A Counter-Blaste to Tobacco* in which he said that smoking tobacco was 'loathsome to the eye, harmful to the brain, dangerous to the lungs'. Why do you think that James I's pamphlet did not stop people smoking?

Tobacco and the law

Tobacco is a **legal drug** but it is so damaging to health that it is illegal for shopkeepers to sell tobacco or cigarettes to young people under the age of 16, even if they are buying them for someone else.

Tobacco addiction
Tobacco is very **addictive**. This means that people who smoke even a few cigarettes a day crave a cigarette if they try to stop smoking. Their bodies need the cigarettes to feel normal.

Cigarette companies and the government know that the younger a person is when they start to smoke, the more likely they are to become addicted. If an 18-year-old does not smoke, they are unlikely to start. Tobacco companies know this and try to target young people. At the same time, the government tries to prevent them. The two groups constantly try to outwit each other.

Every cigarette advertisement and every packet of cigarettes and tobacco must have a government health warning printed on it. In Canada and New Zealand, tobacco advertising is banned altogether.

Smoking is banned in some places because it is dangerous. Petrol can easily be set alight by a match or burning cigarette.

Controlling advertising

The government controls how cigarettes are advertised. The actual laws vary from country to country and in Australia from state to state. In Britain, tobacco advertising is being controlled more and more strictly. At one time cigarettes were widely advertised on television, in magazines, in the cinema and on huge street hoardings. By the year 2000 all open advertising was made illegal and had disappeared. From 2006 cigarette advertising and **sponsorship** will be banned in the European Union.

Think about it

Some people say that tobacco companies do not force people to buy cigarettes and it is up to each person to decide whether they want to smoke. Other people say that it is the duty of government to protect people from harm. Who do you think is responsible for your health?

Did you know?

Fewer people are smoking. In 1972 about half of all British adults smoked, but by 1999 less than a third did. Many smokers had died but many others had given up. Unfortunately there was no fall in the number of young people who took up smoking. About a quarter of British 15-year-olds smoke regularly.

What happens when someone smokes?

Cigarette smoke contains more than 4000 **chemical compounds**. The three main ingredients that harm the body are **tar**, **carbon monoxide** and **nicotine**. When a smoker lights up a cigarette and takes a puff, the smoke passes through the mouth and into the lungs.

Smoke-filled lungs

The hot smoke burns the throat and the delicate lining of the lungs. It irritates the bronchial tubes that lead into the lungs. The body tries to get rid of the smoke by coughing. Even regular smokers tend to cough when they smoke their first cigarette of the day. The tar in cigarettes is black and sticky, like the tar that is laid on roads. It collects in the lungs and the poisonous chemicals it contains are absorbed into the blood.

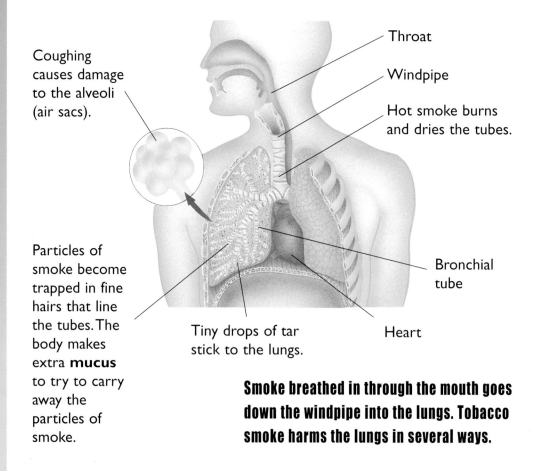

Coughing causes damage to the alveoli (air sacs).

Throat

Windpipe

Hot smoke burns and dries the tubes.

Bronchial tube

Particles of smoke become trapped in fine hairs that line the tubes. The body makes extra **mucus** to try to carry away the particles of smoke.

Tiny drops of tar stick to the lungs.

Heart

Smoke breathed in through the mouth goes down the windpipe into the lungs. Tobacco smoke harms the lungs in several ways.

Damaging the body

Chemicals from the smoke pass through the lining of the lungs and into the blood. Blood usually carries a good supply of vital oxygen to the brain, heart and every **cell** in the body. But the carbon monoxide in the smoke deprives the body of some of the oxygen it needs.

When a person smokes frequently over a long period of time, the continual presence of carbon monoxide in the blood can cause **heart disease**. Nicotine passes into the blood too. It makes the heart beat faster and affects the nerves in the brain.

Did you know?

You might be surprised at some of the chemicals present in cigarette smoke. They include arsenic (a poison used by many infamous murderers); hydrogen cyanide (a gas used to execute people in the United States); ammonia (a chemical used to clean toilets); and formaldehyde (a chemical used to preserve dead specimens).

Smokers may not realize that their clothes and breath sometimes smell of stale cigarettes, just like this ashtray, but other people notice. Regular smokers cannot smell or taste as well as non-smokers can.

How does it feel to smoke?

People who smoke regularly say that smoking a cigarette makes them feel calm and helps them to concentrate. The **chemical** that produces this feeling is **nicotine**.

Jittery and anxious

Nicotine blocks nerve signals in the brain and so makes the smoker feel relaxed, but to overcome the blockage the brain produces extra signals. After a while these extra signals make smokers feel jittery and anxious again, so they light up another cigarette. The smokers say it makes them relax, but in fact it just makes them feel, for a short time, the way a non-smoker feels!

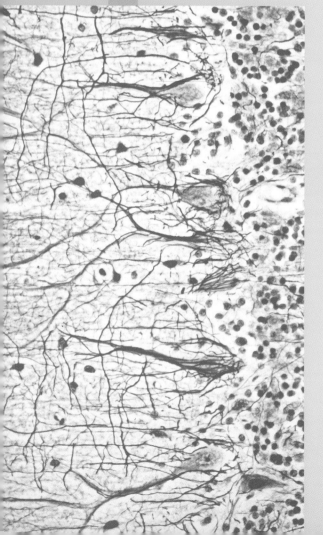

Nicotine addiction

The main problem with nicotine is that it is **addictive**. This means that the body not only gets used to the drug, but needs it to function normally. Someone may start by just smoking one or two cigarettes a day, but soon smokes more. People who smoke cannot last very long without another cigarette. They feel restless and irritable and find it difficult to concentrate on anything else.

Millions of nerve cells pass information from one part of the brain to another. Smoking interferes with the chemical that is responsible for passing on the nerve messages.

Craving for a cigarette

Smoking also becomes a **habit** for many people. Some people get used to having a cigarette at the end of a meal or when they have a cup of tea. They expect to have a cigarette then and their body craves for it. They go on wanting a cigarette until they have one, or do something else and manage to forget about it.

Did you know?

Smoking is expensive. Many regular smokers buy a packet of 20 cigarettes a day. If they saved the money instead, they could buy a new computer game after two weeks, or a CD-player after a month. Smoking just two cigarettes a day costs over £100 a year. Smoking five a day over a smoker's lifetime (which is shorter than most people's lifetimes) would cost as much as a sports car.

Warning: The Surgeon General Has Determined That Cigarette Smoking Is Dangerous to Your Health.

17 mg "tar," 1.0 mg nicotine av. per cigarette, FTC Report Aug. '77

This cigarette advertisement links relaxing in healthy fresh air with smoking a particular brand of cigarettes. It does not tell you that cigarettes make you edgy and pollute the air.

15

Regular smoking

Smoker's cough

Regular smoking damages a person's health. The breathing tubes are lined by fine hairs that protect the lungs by catching dirt and germs. These fine hairs become clogged with particles from tobacco smoke and cannot work properly. The body makes extra **mucus** to try to clear the tubes and the smoker develops a continual cough to help get rid of the mucus. As their lungs and heart work less well, smokers become short of breath. Serious athletes never smoke.

Early deaths

Heavy smokers are often ill and cannot work. They may get **bronchitis** or heart problems. The more a person smokes the greater the damage to their health – about half of all smokers die early due to smoking. Every year it kills about 120,000 people in Britain and about 450,000 smokers in the United States, mainly from **lung cancer** and heart attacks. It is estimated that by 2020, 10 million people will die each year due to tobacco.

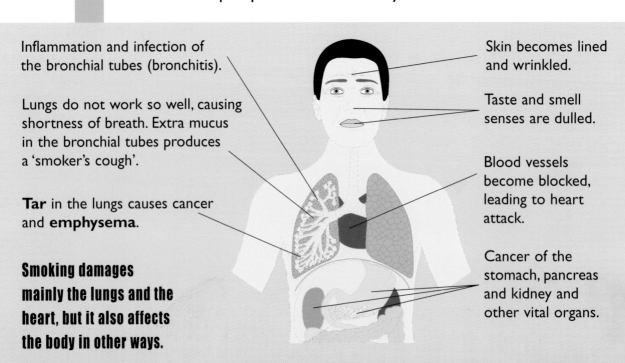

Inflammation and infection of the bronchial tubes (bronchitis).

Lungs do not work so well, causing shortness of breath. Extra mucus in the bronchial tubes produces a 'smoker's cough'.

Tar in the lungs causes cancer and **emphysema**.

Smoking damages mainly the lungs and the heart, but it also affects the body in other ways.

Skin becomes lined and wrinkled.

Taste and smell senses are dulled.

Blood vessels become blocked, leading to heart attack.

Cancer of the stomach, pancreas and kidney and other vital organs.

Fatal illnesses

Tobacco smoke damages the lining of the lungs and can lead to lung cancer and emphysema. About three-quarters of those who die from these long and painful illnesses are smokers.

Carbon monoxide in the blood slowly blocks up the arteries (the tubes that carry blood away from the heart). In extreme cases, people have had their legs amputated because the blood was unable to reach their feet and lower legs so the body tissue in these parts died. But more commonly, blocked arteries in the heart cause a heart attack.

Did you know?

A 60 mg (a thimbleful) of pure **nicotine** taken all at once would probably kill a person. Each cigarette contains 1 mg of nicotine. The reason why people who smoke 60 cigarettes a day do not die straight away is because the body continually breaks down the nicotine and so prevents the fatal dose from accumulating.

The lungs of a smoker (right) are clearly dirty and damaged, compared with the healthy lungs of a non-smoker.

Why do people do it?

Why do people start smoking?
Almost everyone who starts smoking is less than 20 years old, and probably less than 18 years old. They may feel unsure of themselves and think that smoking a cigarette will make them look and feel more confident. They may think that by smoking they will meet people, particularly people of the opposite sex. If a girl likes the look of a boy, she can offer him a cigarette or ask him for a light. Most young people, however, do not smoke and are unlikely to be attracted to someone who does.

Stuck in the past
Young people who start smoking usually do so because they think it makes them more adult. Yet the opposite is true. Although you see many adults smoking, they almost certainly began to smoke when they were teenagers. So smoking is a **habit** left over from their teenage years, not something that they have chosen to do recently.

What do you think this advertisement is trying to say? Tobacco companies claim that they advertise to persuade smokers to buy their brand of cigarette, but most advertisements give the impression that smoking in general is sophisticated.

When we say we have nothing to wear, never try to convince us otherwise.

VIRGINIA SLIMS
It's a _woman_ thing.

© Philip Morris Inc. 1996
8 mg "tar," 0.7 mg nicotine av. per cigarette by FTC method.

SURGEON GENERAL'S WARNING: Smoking Causes Lung Cancer, Heart Disease, Emphysema, And May Complicate Pregnancy.

This Formula 1 car is partly paid for by a tobacco company.

Tobacco companies are not allowed to advertise directly to young people, so they find other ways of appealing to them. Many tobacco companies spend a large amount of money on **sponsorship**. By sponsoring, for example a Formula I car, the company links their name with the excitement of racing. They are also getting their name seen on televisions around the world.

Did you know?

For many years an actor called Wayne McLaren featured in an advertisement for Marlboro cigarettes. He was dressed as a cowboy on horseback in wide, open countryside. He later developed **lung cancer** due to smoking. Some actors who helped to promote cigarettes later toured schools explaining to children why they should not smoke.

Should sponsorship be banned?

From 2006 cigarette advertising and sponsorship will be banned in the European Union. Many people in Europe want cigarette sponsorship to be banned before then, but some sports, such as motor racing, say that they need time to get money from somewhere else first. If sponsorship was banned too soon, international motor races, for example, would just be held in countries where sponsorship is allowed, and Europeans would still see it on television. What do you think should happen?

Passive smoking

Smoking not only damages the smoker's health, it affects the health of people around them, too. Breathing in someone else's tobacco smoke is called **passive smoking**. Second-hand smoke contains many poisonous **chemicals**, including **carbon monoxide**, arsenic, cyanide and radioactive chemicals.

Family and friends suffer

Scientific reports in the 1980s and 90s proved that passive smoking damaged non-smokers' health in much the same way as it did smokers' health. A smoker's family and friends are most likely to suffer. The children of smokers may suffer from **asthma** or have other breathing problems.

Some offices ban smoking inside the building. These office workers have to go outside to have a cigarette.

Banning smoking

In the 1990s non-smokers demanded that they be protected from other people's smoke. Smoking in public places is becoming increasingly unacceptable. Most buses and railway carriages are non-smoking and larger areas in pubs and restaurants are now non-smoking. Smoking is banned altogether on most aircraft and in some cinemas and airports. Many office workers have voluntarily agreed to make their work places smoke-free.

Did you know?

In 1992 a report by the **US Environmental Protection Agency** said that one fifth of asthma attacks in children were a result of the children breathing in second-hand smoke. It also estimated that passive smoking kills 40,000 Americans a year due to **lung cancer** and **heart disease.**

Some restaurants ban smoking altogether. Others separate the restaurant into smoking and non-smoking areas. Non-smoking diners sometimes complain that the smoke drifts across into their non-smoking area.

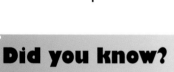

The right to choose

Many smokers say that they have the right to smoke and that governments and other people do not have the right to stop them, even if they damage their bodies. Other people say that they have the right not to breathe in second-hand smoke in public places. What do you think?

Smoking and pregnancy

From mother to baby

There is one group of people who suffer more than others from **passive smoking**. They are babies both before and after they are born. A baby growing in its mother's womb needs food and oxygen like everyone else. It cannot breathe or eat, so the mother breathes and eats for it. Oxygen and digested food in the mother's blood pass through the placenta and the umbilical cord straight into the baby's blood.

Effects on the baby's health

When the mother smokes, the baby's health is affected in several ways. As the mother smokes the cigarette, less oxygen passes into the baby's blood. As a result, smokers are more likely to have a **miscarriage** and tend to have more medical problems during the pregnancy than non-smokers. When the baby is born, it is more likely to be underweight and to need special care and attention. Babies whose mothers smoke are twice as likely to have chest infections as the babies of non-smokers.

An unborn baby is supplied with food and oxygen from its mother's blood.

A smoky home

Babies and young children who live in a smoky atmosphere are more likely to have problems with their ears, lungs and throat. They are more likely to have breathing difficulties. If they suffer from **asthma**, a smoky home will make it worse. Cot deaths, too, are less likely to happen in homes where no one smokes.

A newborn baby needs to breathe clean air. If someone in the family smokes regularly, the baby is more likely to suffer from chest and ear infections.

Who pays?

It is estimated in Britain that treating diseases caused by smoking costs the National Health Service over £1.7 billion. Some people say that smokers should have less priority in hospitals than non-smokers. But smokers in Britain pay in total over £10,000 million **tax** on cigarettes. Should smokers be made to pay extra towards the Health Service?

Did you know?

Every year in Britain more than 17,000 babies and children under 5 years old have to go into hospital because of an illness or condition caused by passive smoking.

Giving up

For people who smoke just one or two cigarettes a day, giving up is not too difficult. Even so, they will probably feel like smoking a cigarette for weeks or months afterwards. People who smoke several cigarettes every day find it much harder to stop.

Making the decision

Many people make up excuses for continuing to smoke. They tell themselves that they are young and will stop smoking when they are older. They do not take into account the fact that it will be no easier then and that they are damaging their health in the meantime. Many other people do stop, but not for long. It takes determination and will power to stop for good.

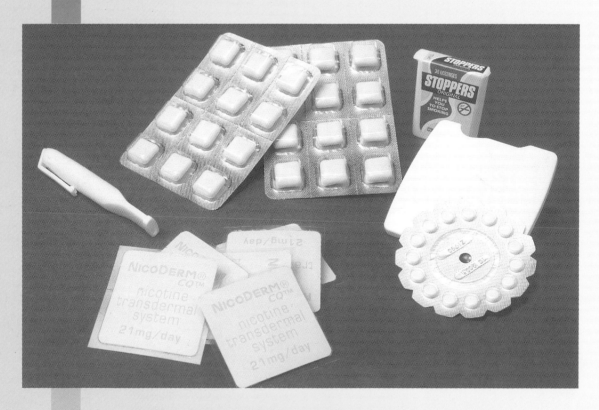

Giving up smoking is not easy, but it is not impossible either. Some people find that products like these, which give them nicotine in another form, help them to stop smoking.

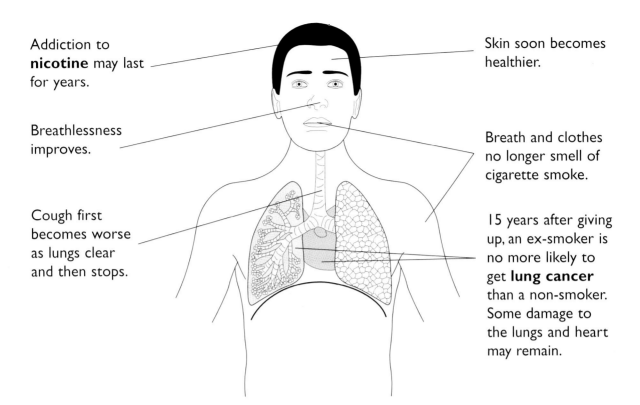

Addiction to **nicotine** may last for years.

Breathlessness improves.

Cough first becomes worse as lungs clear and then stops.

Skin soon becomes healthier.

Breath and clothes no longer smell of cigarette smoke.

15 years after giving up, an ex-smoker is no more likely to get **lung cancer** than a non-smoker. Some damage to the lungs and heart may remain.

Help in giving up

There are many products and techniques that try to make giving up easier. **Acupuncture** helps some people. Saving the money they would have spent on cigarettes and then spending it on something special can help too.

Smokers who give up often have to change many of their other **habits** too. If they are used to having a cigarette at certain times and in certain situations, they have to organize their lives in a different way. There are websites, books and leaflets that offer advice. The best advice, of course, is: 'Don't start in the first place.'

As soon as a smoker gives up the body begins to repair itself, but it may take several years before all the damage is put right.

Did you know?

Thousands of people are giving up smoking. In Britain about 50,000 people give up every year. Each day in the United States about 3500 successfully stop smoking.

Saying no

Reasons for saying no

Many children are worried that if they say no, their friends will think they are stupid and childish. But it is more stupid to start smoking. This book gives you plenty of reasons for saying 'no', such as 'I don't want to damage my lungs'. You can think of other things that you might say, such as 'I don't want to endanger my future career as a great footballer' or 'I don't want to smell like an old ashtray'.

The right choice

But you don't have to give an excuse. Everyone accepts now that smoking damages your health. Why give money to the cigarette companies when you can spend it on something else? If you don't want to smoke then just say so clearly. People are more likely to try to persuade you if they sense that you are unsure.

There are better ways of looking cool than smoking cigarettes – inline skating, for example.

Spending time with your friends is an important part of growing up. Listening to music, talking, cycling and other sports are just a few of the things that you can enjoy together.

Making new friends

If your friends are experimenting with cigarettes, alcohol, or other things you aren't interested in, you should think about whether they are the best friends for you. Friendships are important and it is not always easy to change friends. Nevertheless, try to take up some new interests or activities and you will probably soon widen your circle of friends.

Did you know?

Two-thirds of people who smoke would like to give up. In Britain, nearly 10,000 hospital beds are occupied every day by people who are in hospital because of smoking.

The right to say 'no'

Some people may think it is daring to smoke, but it can take more courage to refuse a cigarette. Why do people encourage non-smokers to try a cigarette? Is it because they want to feel it is okay to smoke?

Dealing with stress

Is smoking the answer?

People who smoke often say that cigarettes make them calm and help them to concentrate. Whenever something stressful or upsetting happens, they reach for a cigarette. Smoking perks them up and calms them down at the same time, but only for a short time. They soon feel restless, anxious and long for another cigarette. This is the effect that **nicotine** has on the brain (see page 14). It is much better to deal with stress in other ways.

Finding ways to cope

Young people can experience a lot of stress. They may feel that they are different from other people. They may fall out with their friends, or find it difficult to make friends. They may not like the way they look and they may want many things in their lives to be different. Sometimes it can help to write down all the things that you are anxious about. Physical exercise will also make you feel better – it helps to reduce tension and stress.

Swimming stretches and relaxes the body. It is a good way to deal with stress and to focus your mind before studying.

Talk about it

One way to deal with stress is to talk to someone you can trust. If you talk to your friends, they may be able to help you or you may discover that they feel the same way as you. You could also talk to an adult, someone in your family perhaps, or a teacher. Most schools have teachers who are there to help you with personal problems.

Did you know?

When people feel stressed, their heart beats faster and their muscles become tense. They may have headaches and find it difficult to sleep at night. Stress can make you feel irritable, moody and anxious.

Exercise keeps you fit and looking your best. It also releases a **chemical** in your brain which makes you feel less anxious or depressed.

Useful contacts

Smoking

Australian Drug foundation – for information write to:
409 King Street, Melbourne 3000, Australia
or telephone: 03 9278 8100
or website: www.adf.org.au

ASH – for free information on smoking and health send
a stamped addressed envelope to:
102 Clifton St, London EC2A 4HW,
email: action.smoking.health@dial.pipex.com
telephone: 020 7739 5902.

Childline – provides free support for children or young
people in trouble or danger:
freephone helpline: 0800 1111.

Direct Line – for counselling:
telephone: Australia 1800 136 385

Drug info Line –
telephone: Victoria 131570 or NSW 02 93612111

Imperial Cancer Research Fund – for information and
advice on cancer:
PO Box 123, Lincoln's Inn Field, London WC2A 3PX.

Quitline – for friendly help and advice on giving
up smoking:
freephone: 0800 002200, open every day 1pm to 9pm.

Glossary

acupuncture a Chinese technique of puncturing the skin with needles to reach nerve areas

addicted unable to give up a habit. Tobacco is addictive because most smokers cannot stop smoking it

asthma tightening of the tubes in the lungs which makes breathing difficult

bronchitis coughing caused when the large tubes in the lungs (called bronchii) become irritated and inflamed

cannabis an illegal drug made from hemp. Cannabis is also called marijuana and hashish.

carbon monoxide a poisonous gas made up of carbon combined with a small amount of oxygen

cell the building block of all living things, including the human body

chemical a substance that is used in chemistry

chemical compound a substance made up of more than one different simple chemical

cured treated to prevent rotting

depressant a substance that slows down the body's reactions and relaxes the muscles

emphysema a serious disease of the lungs which causes the lungs to take in too much air, leading to difficult breathing and coughing

habit something you do regularly without thinking about it and so is hard to stop

hallucinogen a drug that heightens experiences or makes things which are imagined seem real

heart disease damage to the heart which prevents it working properly

illegal drug a drug, such as heroin, LSD or cannabis, which is forbidden by law

legal drug a substance which affects the body but is allowed by law. Medicines, coffee and tea are legal drugs

lung cancer a serious illness in which new cells in the lungs grow uncontrollably

medicines substances which are used to treat or cure illnesses

miscarriage the birth of a baby before it has developed enough to be able to live

mucus thick liquid that protects tubes inside the body

nicotine an addictive substance that is present in tobacco

passive smoking breathing in someone else's tobacco smoke

prescribed advised or ordered by a doctor

sponsorship financial help, often in exchange for advertising

stimulant a substance that speeds up the body

tar thick, black sticky substance made by burning tobacco

tax money paid to the government

Index